# RECORD BUSTERS
# OLYMPICS

## STEPHEN WHITE-THOMSON

WAYLAND
www.waylandbooks.co.uk

First published in Great Britain in 2015
by Wayland

Dewey Number: 796.4'8-dc23
ISBN: 978 0 7502 9542 0
Library ebook ISBN: 978 0 7502 9647 2
10 9 8 7 6 5 4 3 2 1

Wayland
An imprint of
Hachette Children's Group
Part of Hodder & Stoughton
Carmelite House
50 Victoria Embankment
London EC4Y 0DZ

An Hachette UK Company
www.hachette.co.uk

www.hachettechildrens.co.uk

Printed in China

## Abbreviations used:

km/h = kilometres per hour
m = metres
cm = centimetres
ft = feet
in = inches
kg = kilograms

Tricky words are listed in 'But What
Does That Mean?' on page 31.

Produced by White-Thomson Publishing Ltd.

**White-Thomson Publishing Ltd**
www.wtpub.co.uk

Editor: Stephen White-Thomson
Designer: Clare Nicholas
Proofreader/researcher/fact checker:
Izzi Howell
Wayland editor: Annabel Stones

Picture credits:
The author and publisher would like to thank
the following for allowing their pictures to
be reproduced in this publication: Cover Stu
Forster/Getty Images; Getty: p. 4 LIFE Picture
Collection; p. 5 IOC/Allsport; p. 6–7 Bryn
Lennon/Staff; p. 7 Michael Steele/Staff; p. 8–9
David Cannon/Allsport; p. 10 Tommy Hindley/
Professional Sport/Popperfoto; p. 11 Michael
Steele; p. 13 Helen H. Richardson The Denver
Post; p. 14 Staff/AFP; p. 15 Manny Millan/
Sports Illustrated; p. 16 Heinz Kluetmeier/
Sports Illustrated; p. 17 Jeff Siner/Charlotte
Observer/MCT; p. 18 Stu Forster; p. 20 Streeter
Lecka, p. 20–21 Quinn Rooney; p. 22–23 Martin
Bureau/AFP; p. 23 STF/AFP; p. 24–25 Alexander
Hassenstein/Bongarts; p. 25 Popperfoto;
p. 26–27 Cameron Spencer; p. 28–29 Nathaniel
S. Butler/NBAE. Shutterstock: p. 12–13
Songquan Deng/Shutterstock.com

# WHAT'S INSIDE?

# OLYMPIA 776BCE

In 776BCE, a big sporting event was held in Olympia in Greece. People came from all over the Greek world to compete. Even wars were put on hold while the Games lasted.

## FIRST EVER GAMES!

## Can you believe it?

There were events such as chariot racing, running and javelin throwing. Pankration was a vicious mix of wrestling and boxing. There was also a prize for being the best trumpeter!

## WOW!

ONLY GREEK MEN TOOK PART IN THE GAMES, AND THEY ALL PERFORMED NAKED!

Greek wrestlers fighting for prizes.

# ATHENS 1896

The first modern Olympics took place in Athens, Greece. Athletes from 14 countries took part in nine different sports.

Spiridon Louis enters the stadium at the end of the marathon.

## Can you believe it?

It is rumoured that during the marathon race, the Greek runner, Spiridon Louis, was given a shot of brandy and an orange by his girlfriend. He went on to win the race!

# USAIN BOLT

Jamaican sprinter Usain Bolt won the London 2012 100 m in 9.63 seconds, setting an Olympic record. He also became the first man to achieve the 'double double' - winning the 100 m and 200 m in back-to-back Olympics.

## Can you believe it?

Usain's nickname is 'Lightning Bolt', which is not surprising as he can run at almost 36 km/h. He's almost 2 m – 6 ft 5 in – tall, which is very tall for a sprinter.

## WOW!

WHEN HE RETIRES FROM RUNNING, USAIN'S AMBITION IS TO PLAY FOOTBALL FOR MANCHESTER UNITED!

Usain runs the final leg of the 4 x 100 m relay event. The Jamaican team won in a record 36.84 seconds.

# CONTENDERS

Irish sprinter Jason Smyth, who is legally blind, did the 'double double' when he won the T13 100-m and 200-m golds at both the Beijing and London Paralympics. In London, his 100-m time of 10.46 seconds smashed the Olympic and world records!

Jason in action at the 2012 London Paralympics.

# THE USA

The USA lead the overall medal table, having won 2,400 medals in 26 Games: 976 golds, 758 silvers and 666 bronzes.

## Can you believe it?

Of the four people who have won at least nine Olympic gold medals, three of them are American: swimmers Michael Phelps and Mark Spitz, and athlete Carl Lewis.

## CONTENDERS

China has only taken part in nine Olympics but has already won 201 golds, 144 silvers and 128 bronzes. They dominate sports such as table tennis and diving.

**The USA has hosted the Olympics a record four times: St. Louis (1904), Los Angeles (1932 and 1984) and Atlanta (1996).**

Four-time gold medal winner in Los Angeles 1984, Carl Lewis accelerates down the long jump runway.

# WOW!
## 21 COUNTRIES HAVE ONLY WON ONE MEDAL EACH!

# THE BROWNLEES

## WINNING BROTHERS!

Alistair Brownlee (right) won triathlon gold at London 2012 in the record time of 1 hour, 46 minutes and 25 seconds.

The Brownlee brothers compete in the 10 km race. Jonathan won triathlon bronze.

## WOW!

ALISTAIR'S TIME IN THE 10 KM RUN WAS JUST OVER 90 SECONDS SLOWER THAN MO FARAH'S VICTORY IN THE INDIVIDUAL 10 KM!

# THE MCFADDENS

Before a crowd of 80,000 at London 2012, the American sisters, Tatyana and Hannah McFadden, raced each other in the women's 100 m T54 final. It was the first time that sisters had competed together at the Paralympics.

## Can you believe it?

Tatyana won bronze and Hannah came eighth. Tatyana is a 10-time Paralympic medallist. She's won three golds, four silvers and a bronze during her glittering career.

The McFadden sisters warm down after finishing their 100 m race.

11

# BEIJING 2008

On 8 August 2008, 91,000 spectators were treated to a fantastic four-hour-long opening ceremony for the Beijing Games. It cost more than £50 million.

## Can you believe it?

The ceremony started at eight minutes and eight seconds past eight on the eighth day of the eighth month, 2008. Why? Because the number eight is a lucky number in China, signifying prosperity.

## WOW!

30,000 FIREWORKS WERE SET OFF DURING THE CEREMONY!

**Beijing 2008 was the most expensive summer Olympics ever. It cost more than £20 billion.**

# WOW!

AN ESTIMATED RECORD 4.7 BILLION PEOPLE WATCHED THE 2008 GAMES ON TV.

The magnificent 'Bird's Nest' stadium was the centrepiece of the Beijing Olympics.

Chinese children wearing many different national costumes carry the Chinese flag at the opening ceremony.

# NADIA COMĂNECI

## FIRST PERFECT 10!

It's Montreal, 1976. Nadia Comăneci, the Romanian gymnast, performs on the uneven bars. When the results come through, she's scored the first-ever perfect 10!

## Can you believe it?

Nadia was only 14 at the time. At the same Olympics, she scored another six perfect 10s and won three gold medals and one bronze.

Nadia also scored a perfect 10 on the beam.

## CONTENDERS

Olga Korbut was the star of the 1972 Olympics where she won three golds and one silver. She was the first gymnast to do a backward somersault on the beam.

# KERRI STRUG

At Atlanta 1996, the US team of seven gymnasts needed to win the vault to be sure of beating the Russians and winning gold. What happened next?

## Can you believe it?

Kerri was the last US gymnast to compete. On her first vault, she injured her ankle. But she jumped again, and landed perfectly on both feet before collapsing. Because of her bravery, she managed a high score and the US team clinched gold.

Kerri Strug's leg is heavily bandaged as the US team receive their gold medals.

# JACKIE JOYNER-KERSEE

The US athlete Jackie Joyner-Kersee won heptathlon gold in Seoul 1988 and Barcelona 1992, scoring over 7,000 points in each competition. No other heptathlete has ever scored more than 7,000.

## RECORD POINTS TALLY!

## Can you believe it?

In Seoul 1988, Jackie Joyner-Kersee entered the long jump event. She leapt a massive 7.4 m to set a new Olympic long jump record!

Jackie jumps high and long into the record books!

# JESSICA ENNIS

Jessica Ennis won gold in the heptathlon in London 2012, scoring 6955 points, which was a British and Commonwealth record.

Jessica broke the world record in the heptathlon 100 m hurdles in a time of 12.54 seconds.

# WOW!

JESSICA PUT IN 10,000 HOURS OF TRAINING FOR THE 2012 OLYMPICS!

# SAMUEL WANJIRU

## FASTEST MARATHON MAN!

Kenyan Samuel Wanjiru smashed the Olympic marathon record at Beijing 2008 in a time of 2 hours, 6 minutes and 32 seconds.

## Can you believe it?

Wanjiru's time was almost three minutes faster than the next best Olympic time!

## On the other hand...

Shizo Kanakuri took 54 years, 8 months, 6 days, 5 hours, 32 minutes and 20 seconds to finish his marathon. He went missing during the 1912 marathon, and took up the offer to complete it in 1966!

Samuel crosses the finishing tape to take gold in record-shattering time.

# TIKI GELANA

Ethiopian Tiki Gelana won the women's marathon at London 2012 in a record time of 2 hours, 23 minutes and 7 seconds.

## CONTENDERS

British long-distance runner Paula Radcliffe holds the world marathon record of 2 hours, 15 minutes and 25 seconds but has never won a medal in an Olympic marathon.

Tiki celebrates her marathon record as the rain pours down.

# RICARDO BLAS JR.

It's no surprise that Guam's judo heavyweight is called 'the little mountain'. He weighs a massive 218 kg.

## HEAVIEST!

## On the other hand...

17-year-old Japanese gymnast Asuka Teramoto was the shortest (1.36 m) and lightest (30 kg) Olympian at London 2012.

Defying gravity! Asuka performs on the balance beam in the Artistic Gymnastics Women's Team final.

London 2012

Ricardo, on the right, throws his weight around in this heavyweight judo contest.

# WOW!

AT LONDON 2012, RICARDO WAS 42 KG HEAVIER THAN THE FIVE MEMBERS OF THE JAPANESE WOMEN'S GYMNASTIC TEAM!

# MICHAEL PHELPS

## MOST MEDALS EVER!

US swimmer Michael Phelps is the greatest Olympian ever, having bagged 22 medals at three different Olympics. Will his record ever be beaten?

## Can you believe it?

Phelps has won a record total of 18 golds.

## CONTENDERS

Larisa Latynina was a star gymnast from the Soviet Union. From 1956 to 1964, she won 18 medals including nine golds.

22

# WOW!

PHELPS' ARMSPAN IS 2 M, THE SAME WINGSPAN AS A BALD EAGLE, AND 7.5 CM MORE THAN HIS ACTUAL HEIGHT!

Michael powers down the pool in the men's 100 m butterfly final to yet another gold at London 2012.

The man with the golden grin: Michael with his eight golds at Beijing 2008.

# BIRGIT FISCHER

German Birgit Fischer is a kayak sprint specialist. She competed in six Olympics between 1980 and 2004 and won medals in all of them! Her total medal tally is eight golds and three silvers.

## Can you believe it?

In 2004, Birgit Fischer came out of retirement. In a close-fought final, the German foursome beat the favourites, the Hungarians, by 0.2 seconds.

At the end of the Kayak K4 500 m, Birgit was the only one to have the strength to lift up her paddle in triumph!

Steven celebrates another gold for the 'four without coxswain' rowing race in Sydney 2000.

# CONTENDERS

British rower Steven Redgrave has won a gold medal at each of the five Olympics he's taken part in. Of Birgit's sport, he says: "I tried kayaking once and fell in within four seconds!"

# WOW!

BIRGIT WON HER LAST GOLD MEDAL 24 YEARS AFTER SHE'D WON HER FIRST.

# BRITISH CYCLISTS

## SIX IN A ROW!

To reach the final of the women's 3000 m team pursuit at London 2012, British cyclists Laura Trott, Joanna Rowsell and Dani King had to get through six separate rounds. They won each round, setting and breaking their own world records as they went.

## Can you believe it?

Laura went on to clinch a second gold medal in the women's omnium. She won the 500 m time trial stage of the multi-event omnium in an Olympic record time.

# WOW!

JOANNA ROWSELL SUFFERS FROM ALOPECIA, A HAIR-LOSS CONDITION. SHE IS PROUD OF HER BALDNESS AND SAYS IT DRIVES HER TO SUCCEED.

## CONTENDERS

At London 2012, British cycling star Chris Hoy broke two world records on the way to winning the gold in the team sprint. It was Hoy's sixth gold in four Olympics, making him Britain's greatest Olympian.

Laura, Joanna and Dani on their way to breaking the world record in the team pursuit at London 2012.

# THE 'DREAM TEAM'

On their way to winning gold in Barcelona 1992, US basketball superstars scored over 100 points in every game they played; no other Olympic team has done that.

**100+ POINTS EVERY GAME!**

## Can you believe it?

The 'Dream Team' included household names such as Michael Jordan, Larry Bird and 'Magic' Johnson. They beat their 1992 opponents by an average of 43.8 points, another Olympic record.

# WOW!

THEIR OPPONENTS WERE SO IN AWE OF THE 'DREAM TEAM' THAT THEY ASKED FOR THEIR AUTOGRAPHS BEFORE THE MATCHES!

Michael Jordan in action in the Barcelona final against Croatia.

## CONTENDERS

American basketball player Teresa Edwards has won more golds than the 'Dream Team' – the US teams she played in won gold in 1984, 1988, 1996 and 2000, and bronze in 1992.

# WOW!

ONE OF THEIR OPPONENTS SAID OF THE DREAM TEAM: 'THEY WERE ON ANOTHER LEVEL – A GALAXY FAR, FAR AWAY.'

# TEST YOURSELF!

Can you remember all the facts about the Olympic record busters in this book? Test yourself here by answering these questions!

1. Who has won medals in six Olympics?
2. Where were the first Olympics held?
3. Which gymnast was the first to score a perfect 10?
4. What's Usain Bolt's nickname?
5. How many medals has the USA won in all Olympic games?
6. Who has won the most individual medals?
7. How much did the Beijing Olympics cost?
8. Which country does the fastest woman Olympic marathon runner come from?
9. What sport does Laura Trott compete in?
10. How much does the heaviest 2012 Olympian weigh?

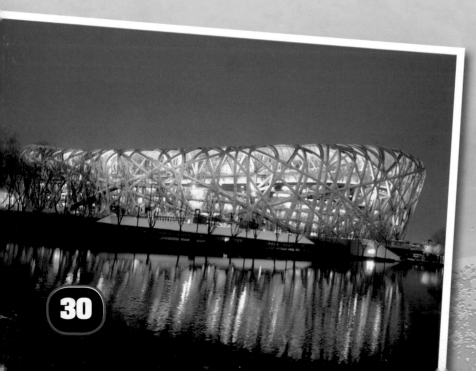

**Answers**

1. Birgit Fischer
2. Olympia, Greece
3. Nadia Comăneci
4. 'Lightning Bolt'
5. 2,400
6. US swimmer, Michael Phelps
7. Approximately £20 billion
8. Ethiopia
9. Cycling
10. 218 kg

# BUT WHAT DOES THAT MEAN?

**accelerate** Start to move more quickly.

**alopecia** Loss of hair, especially from the head, that either happens naturally or is caused by disease.

**balance beam** A thin piece of equipment raised off the floor and used in women's artistic gymnastics.

**butterfly** A swimming stroke in which both arms come forward together and then pull back through the water together while the legs do a kick sometimes known as the 'dolphin kick'.

**dominate** To be very much better than anyone else at a particular sport.

**heptathlete** An athlete who competes in seven different events, including long jump and high jump.

**kayak** A small, narrow boat powered by a double-bladed paddle.

**marathon** A long-distance race over 42.2 km (26 miles and 385 yards).

**omnium** Six different cycling events held over two days.

**Paralympics** An international sporting event in which athletes who have a variety of physical disabilities compete against one another.

**prosperity** Wealth and riches.

**retirement** When you stop competing or doing the job you've done for a long time.

**sprint** When athletes race as fast as they can over a short distance.

**time trial** Sporting events when cyclists race against the clock.

**triathlon** A three-part athletics event including a swim, bicycle ride and a run.

**wingspan** The distance from the tip of one outstretched wing to the tip of the other.

# CHECK IT OUT & INDEX

## Check out these amazing websites!

**http://queenelizabetholympicpark.co.uk**
There's plenty to do and see at the park where the 2012 Olympics were held.

**http://www.paralympic.org**
Official website of the Paralympic Movement.

**http://www.iaaf.org**
Home of World Athletics, the International Association of Athletics Federations.

**http://www.olympic.org**
The official website of the Olympic Movement: great facts, photos and videos of the superstars of Olympic sports.

**http://www.rio2016.com/en**
The official website for the 2016 Olympic Games in Rio de Janeiro, Brazil.

## Index

# RECORD BUSTERS

## Read more amazing titles in the Record Busters series!

### ANIMALS
978 0 7502 6854 7
Blue Whale
African Bush Elephant
Giraffe
Cheetah
Peregrine Falcon
Cosmopolitan Sailfish
Box Jellyfish
Bee Hummingbird
Common Swift
Dung Beetle
Whale Shark
Reticulated Python
Saltwater Crocodile
Polar Bear
Ostrich
Galapagos Giant Tortoise

### BUILDINGS
978 0 7502 7210 0
ADX Florence
Angkor Wat
Boeing Everett Factory
Grand Central Terminal
Burj Khalifa
Ice Hotel
Djenne Grand Mosque
May Day Stadium
Rose Tower
Istana Nurul Iman
Screen Room
Cross Island Chapel
The O2
Great Pyramid of Giza
Suurhusen Church
Yokohama Marine Tower

### MACHINES
978 0 7502 8110 2
The Airbus A380-800
iRobots Roomba
Tmsuk T-52 Enryu
Ecotricity Greenbird
Bagger 293
International Space Station
F1 Powerboat
Mil Mi-26
Kingda Ka
MS Allure of the Seas
Shockwave
NASA Crawler Transporter
Antonov An-225
Tianhe-2
Michigan Micro Mote
Voyager 1

### BUGS
978 0 7502 8109 6
The Goliath Bird Eating Spider
The Australian Termite
The Froghopper
The Monarch Butterfly
The Cicada
The Arctic Wooly Bear Caterpillar
The Mayfly
The Southern Giant Darner
Illacme plenipes
Chan's Megastick
Queen Alexandra's Birdwing
The Hercules Beetle
The Worker Honey Bee
Springtails
The Anopheles Mosquito
The Brazilian Wandering Spider
The Desert Locust

### DINOSAURS
978 0 7502 8861 3
Ankylosaurus
Sauroposeidon
Struthiomimus
Tyrannosaurus Rex
Utahraptor
Quetzalcoatlus
Spinosaurus
Therizinosaurus
Ceratopsians
Argentinosaurus
Elasmosaurus
Troodon
Edmontosaurus

### PEOPLE
978 0 7502 7209 4
Mariusz Pudzianowski
Darren Taylor
David Weichenberger
Fred Grzybowski
Christian Schou
Usain Bolt
Thomas Gregory
Herbert Nitsch
Dave Cornthwaite
Ronaldo
Alia Sabur
Ashrita Furman
Jordan Romero
Jeanne Louise Calment
Mark Zuckerberg
Valeri Polyakov

WAYLAND
www.waylandbooks.co.uk